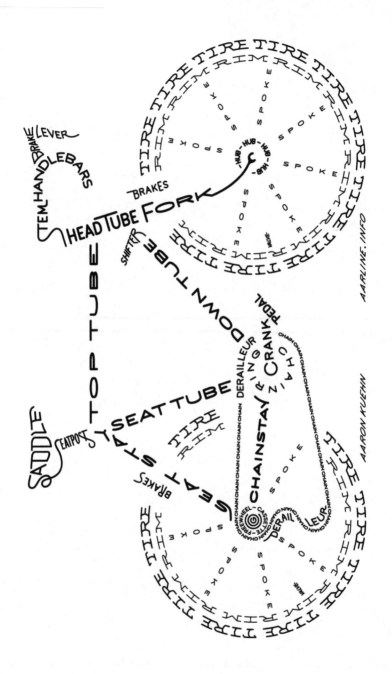

SPOKES

POETRY ON TWO WHEELS

A collection of poems on a cycling theme
to celebrate the
Grand Depart of the Tour de France 2014
from Yorkshire

Otley Word Feast Press
9B Westgate, Otley, West Yorkshire, LS21 3AT

Published by Otley Word Feast Press 2014

Acknowledgements of previous publications of works in this
collection are shown at the end of this book.

ISBN 978-0-9927616-0-8

Printed by
imprintdigital.com, Seychelles Farm, Upton Pyne. Devon. EX5 5YX
info@imprintdigital.com

Contents

Foreword

This collection of poems is brought to you by Otley Word Feast Press to celebrate the *Grand Départ* of the *Tour de France* coming to Yorkshire, including our town, in 2014. Otley is a great place for cyclists, home of the Ron Kitching Cycling Memorabilia Library, the Otley Cycle Races and the Otley Cycling Festival; it is also a town renowned for its poets.

We are especially grateful to the Poet Laureate, Carol Ann Duffy for allowing us to include her poem, 'Lightning Star'. All the other poems were submitted as a result of an open invitation and selected on an anonymous basis. The poets represented here come from Otley, from elsewhere in Yorkshire and from other parts of the UK. Some are famous, some well known locally and others are publishing for the first time. The delights to be found in this collection are many and varied and we hope you find plenty to enjoy.

The publication of this book has been made possible by the unpaid efforts of local poets working in these other guises:

- **Anthologie dirigée par** Jane Kitsen et Sandra Burnett;

- **Textes choisis par** David Andrew, Tony Boltini, Rosalind York, Suzanne McArdle, Gail Mosley, James Nash, Jo Sedgwick, Greg White, Peter White, Noel Whittall;

- **Mise en page** – Peter White;

- **Couverture** – Greg White;

- **Correction d'épreuves** – Rosalind Fairclough

et tous les poètes.

Thank you all.

Jane Kitsen
Chair, Otley Word Feast

Introduction

There's something very human about cycling; as you pedal you get to see things on a manageable scale and distances become more real. The sun shines in your eyes, followed by the rain. The wind lifts you a little and carries you along or it pushes against you like somebody trying to keep you out of a room.

And that's why poetry and cycling go together so well, because poetry is also a great human activity. It begins with breath, as cycling does; it takes us from one place to another, as cycling does; it can have its own language, as cycling certainly can; and there's a sense of achievement when you finish a poem that's comparable to the feeling of elated exhaustion when you get to the top of a hill. And you have to push hard to get a poem started, like you often do when you're just setting off on your bike. You can fall off a poem, too, although poets call that redrafting and it doesn't require plasters.

And now that Yorkshire is very much on the cycling map, with the Grand Depart coming to these parts, this collection can help to put Yorkshire on the Cycling Poetry map, too.

There are poems here about the joys and hardships of cycling, about the equipment and the weather and the companionship and the characters that you get in the sport. There's a real marriage of words and wheels, stanzas and spokes, until it struck me that it's amazing nobody has ever done this before.

I reckon *Spokes* will be the start of a great revival and expansion of cycling poetry, and that every Tour De France will have poems showered on it from now on.

Remember, we did it first here in Yorkshire. Mind you, isn't that always the case?

Ian McMillan

Lori Kiefer

Born cyclist

He couldn't be
a passenger.
He had to feel
the rain.
He was born
with a bicycle
deep in his brain.

Philip Harris

The Fast Commuters

They stood there, the three of them,
motionless
in the green zone
just behind the Advanced Stop Line,
each on one leg, the other clipped-in
ready to push
watching for the change
to amber.
Suddenly they were off, as one.
Smooth, measured, assured,
every pothole known, remembered, avoided.

I saw them up ahead stop on the next red,
and caught them.
For a moment I was one of them.
Standing there, waiting, watching for the change,
in our tight pants, hard hats with holes, swanky shoes, hi-viz
    rucksack covers.
With hands on the hoods, poised, ready,
waiting for the change.
Then we were off, as one.
But it was a headwind that morning.
By Gorton they had a hundred yards on me.
By the time I reached the Mecca at Belle Vue, a quarter of a
    mile.

At nine, they arrive, get changed,
and change.
Office workers now, wheels swapped for screens.
Once cruelly referred to as The Living Dead,
who knows what they do, who they work for,
what difference, what change, they make?
But if dead, then at five they come alive. They change
direction.
They're headed back.
A tailwind now, hunched, on the drops,
twenty-five on the flat, easy.

They're thinking about home.
What's she got for dinner?
A shower, a change, the TV.
Another twenty clocked to add to the week's total.
Then tomorrow, and the next day,
the road, the ride, the same,
no change.

Char March
The love potion flask

All day chalking out patterns;
tacking lapels and kick pleats.

Every evening cranking up through
the gears – a Tag-Relay on the track,

or a Time-Trial into that east wind.
And on a weekend it's an Endurance:

organising the girlfriend
to make up enough sarnies;

to be at the right Feeding Station
at the right time; to mix plenty of sugar

in every water bottle; to hold them just so,
her arm straight; not to flinch

as he trams past gasping, stuffing
sarnie into mouth, spare into back pocket,

bottle into cage. The hours flickering
past in hedgerows. The lanolin – slapped

inside his shorts at dawn – leaking
into the weary saddle till, eleven hours in,

207 miles under his belt, a personal best beckoning
in the final blur of light over Little Fransham,

a slick bend brings him down – loose gravel thick
inside a knee, one elbow a knob of snapped bone,

and her a panicked flag of seersucker
running out of the gloom with a tartan thermos.

Peter Roberts
Saddled by time

I've cycled England 60 years from Vectis to the wall,
Old Kipling might have understood my bike's magnetic call.
The curse of brakes on metal, the whirr of wheels run free
will call this rider to account when time is called on me.

Legs full of pleasure, circle with the crank.
Every turn of pedal is money in the bank.

Sarnies packed in baking foil to feed the hours of happy toil,
I swing my leg across the bar and hear the song of tyre on tar.
The cadence now starts creeping on the rhythm building up
those distant hills are calling me, filling life's sweet cup.

Legs full of pleasure, circle with the crank.
Every turn of pedal is money in the bank.

The summit, when I reached it, filled with nervous pride,
did nothing to prepare me for the downward dizzy ride.
With wind and flies about my face I hurtle down the hill of fate,
I'm ill prepared for going down at such a helter skelter rate.

Legs full of pleasure, circle with the crank.
Every turn of pedal is money in the bank.

In the valley at the end of day, I know there is a pub,
other cyclists resting there like some eccentric hub.
The chat of journeys gone and done and thoughts and hopes of
more,
for some, they know, that 'Father Time' is standing at their
door.

Legs full of pleasure, circle with the crank.
Every turn of pedal is money in the bank.

My final ride has come at last; it won't be any frantic blast.
A gentle wander down the vale of memories both bright and
pale.
The wind is gentle at my back, my saddle soft to seat, my gears
are low, my spirits high
as down the road my fate I ply. To my last beer the pleasures
die.

Legs full of pleasure, circle with the crank.
Every turn of pedal is money in the bank.

Michael Shann
A perfect circle

Leaving Epping, both bikes clean,
we ripped through the forest,
tore it from north to south
with two cuts of zipping tread.

Umber and lemon-ochre. Sunshine
filtered through beech and hornbeam.
Old friends not past trying
something new again.

We traded marriages and jobs
for mud-sputter and puddle-spit.
Got lost. Tonned it down hills
we couldn't see the bottom of.

Then we stopped. A clearing.
A solitary oak's first hard frost.
A perfect circle, flaming yellow,
laid down like the shock

of a summer dress slipped from
shoulders to pool on the floor.
We grinned like young lads
unused to sudden nakedness,

then pedalled on, keeping
a promise to be back before dark,
before the wind got up
and the leaves were squandered.

Michael Brewer
How to ride a penny farthing

First, left foot on the footstep at the back,
then hold the handlebars, so you can steer.
It may seem strange, but you'll soon get the knack.

Push with your right foot, scoot along the track,
climb up the backbone, there's no time for fear.
First, left foot on the footstep at the back.

When you're safe in the saddle, have a crack
at feeling for the pedals, they're quite near.
It may seem strange, but you'll soon get the knack.

If there's a steep hill that you cannot hack,
dismount, until the gradient's less severe.
When stopping, use the footstep at the back.

You're on a High Wheel! Now you can attack
all your speed records, in so high a gear;
it may seem strange, but you'll soon get the knack.

If you should take a tumble, from a lack
of looking where you're going, persevere.
First, left foot on the footstep at the back.
It may seem strange, but you'll soon get the knack.

Carole Bromley
Cycling with Gordon Ramsay

Nightmare. Every ten yards
some reason to swear;
the air was blue with it:

speed bumps, dodgy motorists,
punctures, dogs, crawling traffic,
and me. Always in the wrong gear,

apparently. *Cadence!* he'd shout,
Fucking cadence! Even the view
didn't suit. *Fucking hills!*

*Fuck me! How come there's
more fucking up than fucking down?*
But he made the best sandwiches.

Anne Caldwell
Raleigh Bikes, 1976

The summer stretches out before us like
a song. A farm dog barks, a blackbird scuttles
underneath the privet hedge. We're freckled,
fit as whippets, peddling up the narrow
road with passing places. We skirt The Edge
where millstone grit butts up against the Cheshire
moss. We know that days will never be
this clear. Somewhere down below us,

Lindow Man lies flat-faced in the peat,
a noose about his neck and somewhere up
the ridge our friend will lose his grip and crack
his skull. For now, we have a den, an oak
to climb, two cans of Sprite. We reach the summit,
turn downhill to face a wall of heat.

Zoe Walkington
Mr. Pinarello

There's this one bloke from our club –
you'll know him. He's the one with the *Pinarello*.
Him with the *Thule* roof rack,
and the *Castelli* speed suit,
and the helmet lighter and stronger than kryptonite.
He's the one with the carbon bike frame, carbon tri-bars,
    carbon shoes.

So he goes on this ride, one Sunday, sets off at six.
Leaves his nice warm bed, hears the chaffinches, and he's off
    and away.
Thinks he'll get to Hawes, maybe further.

But the skies turn to acrimony,
and the wind knocks him sideways,
and IT IS ALL UPHILL,
and the roads are glass and razor wire,
and his inner tubes are ribbons,
and the carbon turns to lead,
and his rear mech snags a fallen tree,
and the tarmac sucks his wheel rims,
so he sinks into the road,
where he grinds to a halt,
with his knees joined to his elbows.

Rumour has it he is still there,
now rusted to that hill.
His hair and ears still growing
so his helmet is a vice now
with his skin grown over his *Mavic* shoes
and his bones turned into carbon.

Alwyn Marriage

Lycra

I hear the hiss of tyre on tarmac
approaching fast before he comes in view,
detect a change of frequency, whiz
turning surreptitiously to hum,
as suddenly, before I know it, the close-fitting
blue and yellow backside has flashed past.

Lithe, lean and lycra-clad
he clings to handlebars and climbs
over high mountain passes,
lungs expanding with the strain,
then saved by the exhilaration of free fall
as he descends again.

Held by traction I submit
to the attraction of that muscular behind.
Tight, taut and masculine in flight,
his receding figure smooth and streamlined,
catching in the light
the rippling of a single muscle
stretched right to the winning post.

Norman Hadley
Drought's end

Normality has been restored
For northern hills are wet once more
And cyclists sink with gratitude
To axle-depth in peaty ooze;
Their speckled faces split by grins
To find the dust gone with the wind.

And even if the skylarks laugh
To mock the slowness of their progress
They don't mind, for riders know
That love is only pain if unrequited, so
For those who love
The Earth and long to cling onto
This mucky gem, it's good that earth
Should also want to cling to them.

Char March

The oxygen of words and wheels

This is the moor where skylarks mock Vaughan Williams
and curlews' throats bubble with peaty watermusic
and, when I stop pedalling and listen hard, I can hear
Cathy's keenings drifting through the spring air
light as dandelion clocks – and as piercing as hail.

My wheels blur on cobbles into the brass bands
and flags as the railway children come to life again
– emerging like wraiths through whuffs of steam.
Then slogging up and over the ridge of millstone grit and
windfarms, I'm blown – rims hot with braking – into the valley

of hippies and clogs, where artists and hill-farmers,
ex-millworkers, Reiki healers, playwrights
and the largest lesbian community in Britain
make the best multi-grain organic mix ever!
A true rainbow nation of passion for our town.

In my lowest gears, I creak up to Heptonstall
where Sylvia lies in the fierce flames of her talent
above Hebden Water's wooded gouge that she
and Hughes made sing with their poetry.
And I freewheel, derailleur in sore need of WD40,

back to the Brontë moors
… to listen for Heathcliff.

Brenda Cromwell

Le Tour d'Otley

Sithee lads, je pense that nous
Should get oursens out on la rue,
And ride nos bicyclettes à town,
To see tout ce qui's goin' down.
On dit qu'un race is on its way,
And should be ici, any day.
Ee bah gum, it should be bon
Tha knows, 'cos all these fellers sont
Les plus rapides on racin' bikes –
Peut-être, that's not countin' Tykes,
'Cos we'd show 'em a thing or deux
If we could ride along un peu.
But, quelle domage, that's not allowed,
So nous devrons just join wi' t' crowd
And wave nos drapeaux as they pass
Reconnaissant their speed and class.
Et puis, we'll have un pint ou three
En une local 'ostelry.
And when they're braggin', one fine jour,
About the day le mighty Tour
de France came to our petite ville,
We'll smile à lui, and then reveal,
Avec nos têtes 'eld 'igh in t'air,
"Aye lads – we know, 'cos we were there!"

Brian Clark
My Tour

I climb and climb these limestone crags
king of a polka dot dream
conquering one in four after one in four
a lone breakaway, my name on the road.

 Allez, allez, allez!

My Tour began with Brian Robinson and Tom
club runs when the bunch was the *peloton*
sprints for village signs which I never won
but up Yorkshire's moors and cols, I was *champion*.

Thinks he's Charly Gaul, they said — and I was
and also Frederico Bahamontes
sometimes Contador, Jalabert or Virenque
did they too suffer such agonies of bonk?

Heroes of the greatest race I'd never see
fought over roads five times higher than these —
Buttertubs Pass was my *hors catégorie*.
So with not much hope I backed *le bid*.

Et maintenant, c'est arrivé: le Tour de France

and when the sheep return, this road I ride
up hill down dale will never be the same;
my dream will mean much more
when I come back to ride my Tour.

Janet Lancaster
Get the T-shirts

Cheer, cheer, cycling fans!
Tour de France in God's own land:
Polka Dot, come yam!

Pump, pump, Yorkshire heart!
Leave the bunch and beat the clock –
wear that *maillot vert!*

Spin legs! Rain or sun –
sprint high moor to dry-stone dale,
win that *maillot jaune!*

Steph Shields
Badger in a yellow jersey

Yes I saw Bernard Hinault
twenty-eight years ago,
or more. He led the Tour
at some point in between
the Alpes Maritime
and Aveyron – I can't be sure –
for the mind clouds over time
but the vision stays so pure.
A chance encounter –
a sun-baked verge, a coke,
an irresistible urge to see,
to witness. Oh the commotion:
the horns, the clattering cavalcade;
goody bags flung at the crowd,
hats, visors, balloons and gum.
Then a stillness – a lull in the fun.
Police outriders – here they come.
Bernard Hinault, Greg Lemond,
the leaders, then the peloton.
The flash of spokes like silver fish,
the faces taut with sheer endeavour,
bronze legs, sinew, muscle –
the beauty of bike and limb together,
a migration of birds on the wing.
I couldn't help but cheer them on.

Then the Broom Wagon. They were gone.
The silence was one of loss.
I'd waited six hours for Bernard Hinault.
He'd passed, like life, in a blink,
leaving me like Toad on the road –
so desperate to ride in the peloton.

Footnote: Bernard Hinault, 'The Badger', won the Tour de France five times.

Wendy Pratt
Black Beauty

Retired to *Eden Camp**, 'Black Beauty',
my mother's bike, props up a fake bomb shelter.
No longer plagued by the intense futility
of age; to drive forward in a crazy helter-
skelter of comparison, trying to fit in;
to match the whippet fit of racers, or stunt
bikes — the BMX bravery, or denim
dreams of eighties teens, 'Beauty' is defunct.
Though I never thought to question her age, the way
she turned herself over with squeaking, black springs;
leather seat worn to a blush, a spray
of produce in her wicker basket, the sweet 'ping'
of an old bike bell will find me searching the drive
for my mother's back, a soft movement, now retired.

*Eden Camp – A Modern History themed museum, North Yorkshire

Julie Mellor
Here

Where the road stops at the rim of the world,
past the house where my grandmother
cooked for twenty years on a Primus stove

at the top of the cellar steps, the road
where my father won the slow bike race
in 1953, where our uncles had biblical names,

Nicodemus, Diadorus, and our aunt was unrelated,
an evacuee who never went home, where family
is still family, though most are long gone.

Carol Ann Duffy
Lightning Star
for May Duffy and her twelve grandchildren

I run at Lightning Star
and mount her back in one smooth jump;
then gallop her down Rising Brook,
wind in my face.
My pigtails thump.

My trusty steed.
I bend low to her ear
as trees rush by in camouflage.
We fly,
her coconut hooves racing with my heart
towards Moss Pit.

My piebald mount.
My equine brave.
My speed of light.
My warrior.
My Lightning Star.

It isn't far
to where we live –
21 Poplar Way –
so I slow down
as we approach the giant trees
which guard our neat estate.
I'm saddle-sore.
I stand up in my stirrups.

Time for bed.
I feel my horse's handlebars against my knees.
I hear my horse's neighing in my head.

Fiona Ritchie Walker
Time trial

Dad is head down into the wind,
everything black and white.
Behind him, spectators' legs blur.
He's 21, all the road's ahead.

It's 1947 and he's powering
bamboo wheels, double-butted spokes,
tubular tyres, a spare on the back.

He's on the rivet, ready
to suspend history
beside the wall clock in the sun lounge,
to smooth pedal over his daughter's head,
towards his grandson's shoulders.

Gail Mosley

At the first house I remember

a path led down past the apple-tree swing
to an old out-building
where my father wheeled me, perched on his handle-bars,
when he came home for tea.

Drawn there again, to the worn stone step,
the blistery door that creaked,
I'd steal in, petrified
as birds in commotion fluttered out.

I remember the smell of bicycle oil,
alarm at the cling of cobwebs,
the rasp of my crepe-soled sandals
quartering the floor.

Birds and spiders and oily dust
were no bar to the prize I was after
 – another look at the pedal-car
left to rust by the owners before.

I remember the sharpness of flaking metal
and knowing I mustn't
but climbing inside
and going nowhere.

Wanda Phillips
After the night shift

Once, I thought I heard my Dad
coming home at dawn; heard
the pitch and squeal, the patter of
his bike on terracotta hall tiles.

Mum would scrub them on a Saturday,
muttering at the tyre tracks, spills of oil.
Dad whistled on those mornings, or sang
with a one-two-three, waltzing her around
the kitchen, dancing her protests away.

Sunday evenings, he worked in the bike shed,
fixing chains, greasing brakes; I helped too:
balancing his bicycle clips, like giant
hoops of gold, upon the handlebars,
ready for Monday.

Julie Mellor
The collector

He owned a pair of calfskin cycling shoes
from the sixties, a bloom on the leather
like the dusting on a black grape,

a pair of running shoes worn by Chataway
during the 4 minute mile (no matter
that Bannister did it in 3 minutes 59)

and a pair of wooden pattens
that once belonged to Emily Brontë
to keep her feet off the stone-flagged floors,

but most of all he wanted Henry VIII's
tennis shoes, felted wool, listed
in the Royal Accounts, perfect

in their own right, and seen by some
as the prototype for all that was to follow:
Puma Ibizas, Adidas Blue Strikes,

those iconic chequerboard Vans.

T. Boltini

Facts in a nutshell (music by Canned Heat)

Sir Walter Raleigh, inventor of the famous bicycle
as every schoolboy knows, was a very chivalrous man:
he laid his bicycle down once, didn't he just, in a deep puddle
so Anne Boleyn[1] could hop across without getting her frock wet.

But as history later began to take hold and gather pace
Disraeli invented gears which improved things a lot. But please
    note that

no matter how fast you are entitled to pedal with new
    technology
you are not permitted in the third lane of our modern
    motorway system

which owes so much to the work of kindly Doctor Beeching, a
    surgeon
whose powders by the way are still available today, and legal,

while the moreish pills that help you zip up big steep hills
are frowned upon as dangerous. Rightly so. Indeed one could
    do worse

than introduce the young to *Amphetamine Annie,* that never-
    to-be-forgotten
song of the sixties with its tirelessly sapient chorus: "Speed
    Kills".

---

[1] or it could have been Marie-Antoinette

Helen Kay
Diagnosis

How can anything but good pour
from this sun? The purring spokes score

straight, firm shadows on the path,
spinning gravel, strimming grass.

The breaking egg of May paints
stripes, which slice the pizza lane.

All winter we coped without
lines. The bike which slithered, out

of touch with itself, now delivers
me to the liquid light of answers,

definitions we can see and deal
with, shadows which set us free.

Janet Lancaster
Life cycle

Mobo-horse trundles over concrete.
Small arms hug its painted metal mane;
toddler scuffs her soft-shod feet.

*

Glansychan Park. Brand-new trike.
Dad pulls on a rope to slow her down.
She rings bell, pedals, learns to brake.

*

She scoots and scoots on solid wheels,
right foot pushes, right heel brakes,
Triang's worn drum bites and squeals.

*

Eighteen, never had a bike – *Too risky riding one, round yer!*
Four pounds buys an *All Spare Parts*, with basket but no gears
and flopping lever brakes: a real sit-up-and-beggar.

Outside college, Collier Road, flat and little traffic.
Pedal hard! shouts breathless Mick, *Faster, that's it, faster!*
She speeds ahead, yells *Don't let go! Yes! This feels terrific!*

not knowing she is solo, then wobbles, topples, glancing back!
Alone in quiet cul-de-sac, she heaves off from a kerbstone,
tries to keep her balance – even over bumps and cracks.

*

She sits astride a pink-framed Raleigh racer.
Birthday gift – from husband, daughter, son:
cable brakes, two chain-wheels, *derailleurs*.

Freewheeling the descent from Hambleton,
head low, she craves wind in her hair, powers
pedals, swooshes down the straight to Egleton.

*

Perched on her Dawes, watch Nanna plod –
broad foam saddle, chain-guard, *Nice low gears*,
helmet on head, panniers plump with milk, fruit, bread!

Sandra Burnett
Lesson

We wheel your birthday present to the park,
a safe place to learn the art of balance.

Minus stabilizers I steady the bike while you,
biting your bottom lip, struggle to sit on the saddle.

I say,
> *Look straight ahead.*
> *Grip the handlebars.*
> *Push on the pedals.*

I hold on longer than I should and have to ignore
my urge to sprint, catch you up

as your pace quickens. When you wobble, steer
a wild course my heart brakes.

You remembered everything I said,
never looked back.

Mark Newberry
Lycra-clad loony

I was cycling along carefully, mentally flossing,
When I saw straight ahead a pedestrian crossing;
But if you are uncertain what I am about,
Let me remove any shadow of doubt.

I refer to the facility supplied by the law
That's meant to give sensible foot folk the floor;
By chance as it happened − and looking at a loss −
At that moment such a person seemed likely to cross.

A quick look behind me... the highway was clear...
I braked to a crawl and changed down a gear;
But the solitary pedestrian (it's always just one!)
Seemed set to dismiss me and allow me a run.

Fiddling in pockets... examining a purse,
Looking the victim of a mugging or worse,
It was apparent to me that I was ignored
But cycling on slowly I found myself floored!

Without any warning (forgive my wry laugh),
The pedestrian ran into the road – and my path.
We fell in a tangle − unharmed but in shock,
Before tottering to our feet and trying to take stock.

The words that assailed me, I recall to this day:
"You lycra-clad loony, you're supposed to give way!"

Noel Whittall
Do what like what?

"Do you always do it like that?" said Ken.
We were six, if you include Jason's wife
riding stoker on their tandem.
"Do what like what?"
The others astride and ready for off.
Ahead of Ken were Mark and Gerry
all left feet on the kerbstone
right knees bent, right shoes already
tensed on the pedals.
"Do what like what?"
"Get on from the right. Are you left-handed?"
"No, I just always get on from this side."
"Wow, that's weird ..." Ken's words hung
and we pedalled away.
All that afternoon as I rode
beside verges where late
daffodils gave way to bluebells
and my lungs gasped up the hills
I thought about something
I had never, ever, considered before.

Ilse Pedler

The dogs that chase bicycles wheels

stare out of windows,
checking the boundaries
    checking the boundaries.

They have territories to protect,
            circling
                from the backs of sofas
        to front doors,
                to kitchens,
whole worlds held in their flat eyes.

Postmen breach defences,
dropping offerings
to be bitten, ripped and pissed on.

Straining to a point always
just in front of their noses,
the click
    clicking of bicycle wheels
tricking them into the frenzy of a chase
for the white scut of a rabbit.

Unceasingly they scout crowded horizons
for what is not there,
  will never be there.

Allen Ashley
Back on the bike

My Dad pulls on the handlebars,
my cousin holds the seat.
They've told me just go with the flow
and pedal with my feet.
It's Grandma's overgrown back yard
full of weeds and rubble;
I'm three years old, or maybe four,
they'll help me if I tumble.
– Just get back on the bike.

A later bike is second-hand,
the saddle's thin and sharp.
I'm riding like an idiot
around my local park.
No helmet, no proficiency,
no knowledge of the gears.
There's dog mess and some tiny stones –
it's bound to end in tears.
– Just get back on the bike.

Once you can swim, it's always there
when breast stroke is called for;
and bike riding's a lifelong skill –
extend the metaphor.
This world is full of deep potholes
and progress never sure;
you'll get knocked back, you'll get knocked down,
but still return for more.
– Just get back on the bike.

Derailed, debagged and near destroyed
by setback, fuss and haggle.
Stay true to that much younger self
who settled on the saddle.
Apply this rule to every sphere
of tribulating life:
you lost that job, your poem bounced,
you've argued with your wife.
— Just get back on the bike.

Rosalind York
Top of the Hill

You are ten
and summer coming.
Your left foot on the pedal,
your right on the ground ready
to push. You push.

The world rolls
   under you, cranked
      by forces you don't understand,
         the road flares behind you like the trail of a jet,
        the air tears in two,
         lets you through,
          the wind grazes your arms,
          makes your eyes pour,
          the camber leans
           into you, the frame
           tilts the horizon
             to the edge of catastrophe,
            you compensate.

          You stay in the saddle. You don't brake.
          Next time you'll ride without hands.

Geraldine Clarkson
Madonna of the Pedals

She has Russian legs, the postman says,
balletic, terrific, with the Volga streaming
in her veins.

He saves her packets till last, touching
cinderellas, horsemen, athletes, lovers,
astronauts — stamps like holy seals.

He fingers the precious
bulk; heaves his tandem against her
greystone wall, to which ivy clings

pillion. Always sends up a prayer
(St Christopher!)
before he knocks.

Great brassy icon
towers in the entrance. Haloed.
He lifts his offering: votive; postmarked.

Pat Borthwick
Freewheeling

Two uniformed schoolgirls
brake, then slip from their saddles
to linger at the wire mesh fence.
His chickens scratch-peck-croon.

Inside the wooden hut
he prepares their mash,
counts and washes eggs,
fingers through magazines.

Quarter past four every day
he comes out to greet them.
Stop and talk?
Their tongues are on heat.

They always stop and talk,
lean their 'eleven plus' racers
against his sit-up-and-beg,
test newly hatched words.

They watch his eyes fumble.
They've just chafed down ropes
or drawn clay up on the wheel.
Earlier, they shortened their ties.

Come and look at my pictures.
I want you to see something.
But the girls remount and pedal away.
'Perhaps tomorrow,' they say

before they're out of the saddle
and down the cinder track,
swinging their sleek frames this way,
then that. Gathering momentum.

Julie Corbett

Before Lighting up Time
(for the Ladies of the Lonsdale Breeze)

spare batteries, waterproofs, helmets,
a discussion on the merits of gel seats
and eight women move off from the park
the route firmly held in two heads
barriers, potholes, loose gravel
a cycle path and quiet roads
and eight women pedalling two by two
like a long vehicle commanding the road
a boy shouts out, look at them
the Tour de France here in 'ull
no flattery there we are the bees knees
as we ride to be back before dark.

Suzanne McArdle
Cycling

I'm like a highlighted word
in my bright yellow vest.
Motorists can't miss me as
I pedal quick with work to get to,
insect helmet on my head,
squeezing me safe, making me sexless.

A girl passes in shorts and tee.
The sun lights up the streamer
of her hair. I half-remember her.
The motorists see her too –
one toots. A young man whistles.
She smiles, adjusts her duffel-bag,
speeds off to her tutorial.

Joanna Sedgwick
Freewheeling

The cycle dealer
had a sign above his shop
HONEST MACHINES AT HONEST PRICES

But honest women's legs
were hidden beneath layers of heavy skirts;
impossible to straddle a bicycle!

And yet women were falling in love
with this new transportation,
so much in love
they dropped their petticoats,
ribbons, parasols, chiffons,
bonnets, bustles, bodices,
stockings, capes, furs, fans, corsets
and found themselves freewheeling,
lungs expanding in the downhill rush.

Bruce Barnes
Bicycle chain haiku

dry chain, try rag and chain
oil, oiled chain, oily hands,
dry washed hands on rag

save fresh towel from
extra oily chain, use rag
for oiled fingers.

James Nash
towpath

I'm racing to beat the twilight
as it hangs itself like damp washing
in the trees
and the swans on the water
float whiter than at any other time.
My wheels bump and whirr a commentary
on my journey into night
and one star gleams
over the abbey's ragged walls.

I'm racing to beat the twilight
alone
except for the last fisherman
packing up his rods and gear;
next week the year slips a cog
and changes
and he falls away behind me
into the gathering dusk.

I'm racing to beat the twilight
and as it darkens
naked men and women
seem to march
around me in slow columns.
I see
their glazed flesh,
upper bodies catching the remaining light,
lips and nipples

dark flowers
frozen in the bud.
I hear
the sighing wind-band of their breathing,
the soft percussion of their feet.
my light bobs its beam ahead,
illuminating
the remaining path.

Rennie Parker

Marvellous

I'm carrying this one −
Not too heavy, stable grip.
The salesman hooked me out from his corrugated shed
This one's about your size, he said.

I stood there rattling with nerves. It's been two years
She'll notice my gone tyres -
I'll be back with the muscular lads and their steroid frames
Their trigger-happy useless gears.

Now she looks at my neat luggage rack
The sturdy-yet-unobtrusive-alloy-propstand (very useful)
Turns sideways. Doesn't want to say this is it.
I'll take a spin round the yard, she says
Ten minutes later we're going home.

Me, I know I'm perfect
A real Lincolnshire bike from the real Brigg factory.
You can forget your anorexic racers, they're all speed speed
    speed
No intelligence to speak of.
What you want is a true road companion
An extra pair of braze-ons.
She didn't have to do a thing:
I'm exactly the right size.

Last year when some hopped-up kids tried to steal me
I wouldn't go.
Her flashlight ranged the field at 2 a.m., convinced I was still
    there.
I shone out from the ditch where I was thrown –
Not a scratch was on my frame.

When you find one, hang on.
This one levers my tyres off so carefully
You'd think I was plated in 18-carat gold.
And now she's done my bearings with Eezi-Grease
You can't hear me coming at all.

Some of us never go further than town
But I've done Northumberland, gone racing down hills
Made friends with old walls
While she goes off looking at some boring historical stuff
A museum, say, or that 'art'.

She tells me it's Holland next year, and I can't wait -
Those big Dutch guys with their continental kling-klong bells.
I wouldn't mind a tangle....
Marvellous.

Don't worry, I'm not leaving.
She's exactly the right size.

Peter R White
The Cambridge Corral

Metallic horns on skeletal frames;
air compressed in straining rings
to cushion bespoke hooves.
Tier on tier of patient steeds
hobbled in combination
at the hitching rails,
remaining at their station,
straining at their chains,
cogs agog, waiting for trains
to deliver commuters.

Greg White
Unfaithful

You were made for me, you know;
Your frame the perfect size.
Wherever the two of us would go,
I'd sense the envious eyes
Of all around, our graceful flow
Evoking jealous sighs.

I dressed you in the latest gear,
Top-of-the-range expensive stuff.
I cared so much for you but, Dear,
You cleared off with the first scruffy
Type who chanced his luck. It's clear
I wasn't good enough

For you, and you're in pieces now,
Or re-sprayed in some garish hue
That doesn't suit, and no doubt
Often left out wet and barely lubed.
My only solace is your frame, suited
To my stubby shanks, will be too

Short for him and harm his back,
And for this comfort I give thanks.

John Hepworth

On The Bicycle Typogram of Aaron Kuehn:
An approximate sonnet, mentioning the parts named in that beautiful illustration.

*Acknowledgement (g-rudge-ing) : Mr W.S. from near Coventry wrote sonnets
far better than this – but did he know how to put one wheel in front of another?*

Can we compare ought to a cycling day?
What has more top-tube and more derailleur?
Rough winds do shake the fork, rim and chain stay,
And handlebar stems have all too short a term.
Sometime too hard a saddle on seat-post shines,
And often is the gilded paint-job dimmed,
And every tire from firm sometime declines –
By thorn, or nature's changing course enleaked.
But pedaling's eternal lever shall not fail,
Nor lose freewheel, chain-ring or valve;
Nor shall skip-trucks brag they made you use your brake
When in eternal wheels thy hubs hold true.
So long as we of seat-tube, shifter, seat-stay, head-tube spoke
Shone hope none would downtube the crank who wrote this joke.

Note: Aaron Kuehn's Bicycle Typogram *forms the frontispiece of this book*

Cristina Archetti
Urban mythology

A biomechanical assemblage
stalking asphalt
with neither limbs nor legs
but rolling vulcanised rubber fangs
powered by steel wires,
and fast-twitch fibre.

Janus-faced
hunter of distance
harvester of pain
lactic acid trader
chiseller of fatigue.
Who is this magician of rehydration?

An avant-garde artist
painting tarmac-veiled canvas
with water and rare minerals
— ephemeral oeuvres
only trained eyes
can appraise.

Cyborg of the road,
carbon-framed centaur,
to the casual observer
man with a bike.

Jane Kite
Wheelie

one hoisted skyward
the other rolls the world
a truce with gravity

The Poets

Cristina Archetti is Senior Lecturer in Politics and Media at the University of Salford. Despite having published extensively in academia, she has only very recently (and somehow accidentally) discovered the joys of creative writing. The first story she ever wrote, 'Distances', was published in *LS13: A New Generation of Leeds Writers*.

Allen Ashley is a London-based author, prize-winning poet and award-winning editor. As a tutor, he runs several writing groups including Clockhouse London Writers. His poetry has appeared in *The BFS Journal* and *Jupiter SF*. His latest book is as editor of *Astrologica: Stories of the Zodiac* (Alchemy Press, 2013).

Bruce Barnes is on the MA Writing course at Sheffield Hallam. His poems have appeared in various magazines, including *Pennine Platform*. If he is very lucky he wins prizes in poetry competitions. He is a member of the Bradford-based poetry group, Beehive Poets.

In the last hour before the deadline for this Personal Profile, **T. Boltini** says he wrote about thirty, but met a different chap in every one. "Peter White wrote a good one for me on a scrap of paper this afternoon" he says, "but I must have left it in a pub somewhere."

Pat Borthwick is working on her fourth full collection and has won many prestigious prizes for her poetry. She has twice been awarded an International Writers' Hawthornden Fellowship and is a founder member and former chair of NAWE (The National Association of Writers in Education).

Michael Brewer rode a penny farthing in the Jersey Battle of Flowers procession in 1954, but now lives in Groby, in Leicestershire. He has had several poems published, but over the last four years has concentrated on performing his own work at open mic sessions in Leicester.

Carole Bromley lives in York where she is a Creative Writing tutor at the University. Her first collection, *A Guided Tour of the Ice House*, was published by Smith/Doorstop Books, Sheffield in 2011. She loves cycling but usually pushes the bike uphill.

Sandra Burnett lives in Otley and divides her spare time between poetry and cycling. When cycling she prefers to avoid right turns and uphills. She endeavours to be more adventurous with poetry.

Anne Caldwell is an award-winning poet who spent her childhood cycling around Cheshire and is now based in Hebden Bridge. She works for the National Association of Writers in Education. Her collection is *Talking with the Dead* (Cinnamon Press, 2011).

Brian Clark is a writer and international award-winning poet, was a Yorkshire Post journalist, worked in television and film production with the BBC and others, and has always been a keen cyclist and follower of the Tour de France.

Geraldine Clarkson's poems have appeared in *Poetry Review*, *Tears in the Fence*, *Shearsman*, *Iota*, *Envoi*, and *Orbis*. Two of her prose poems were included in *This Line is Not for Turning: An Anthology of Contemporary British Prose Poetry* (Cinnamon, 2011).

Julie Corbett lives in Hull. She has been published in various magazines and anthologies and is currently *Poet at Burton Constable Hall*.

Originally from Leeds, **Brenda Cromwell** has lived in Burley-in-Wharfedale for 28 years. She is a member of The Courthouse Writers and particularly enjoys writing humorous verse and prose.

Carol Ann Duffy lives in Manchester, where she is Professor and Creative Director of the Writing School at Manchester Metropolitan University. She has written for both children and adults, and her poetry has received many awards, including the Signal Prize for Children's Verse, the Whitbread and Forward Prizes, and the Lannan and E. M. Forster Prize in America. In 2005, she won the T. S. Eliot Prize for *Rapture*. In 2009, she was appointed Poet Laureate.

Norman Hadley is a cycling poet in thrall to the cadence of both disciplines. He has produced five poetry collections, two novels and an anthology of short stories. Find out more about the writing at normanhadley.com and the cycling at pedalnorth.com.

A lifelong bike rider, **Philip Harris** loves the freedom and joy cycling gives. He often finds inspiration for his poetry when out riding.

Despite dividing his time between Otley and Leeds, bookseller and writer **John Hepworth** hasn't owned a bike since 1980, nor ridden one for 20 years or so. Nevertheless an unbreakable thread of affection connects him to the two-wheeled transport of his teenage endeavours.

Jane Kite lives in Otley, a town renowned for its poets.

Helen Kay is an emerging poet from Nantwich, Cheshire, beginning to be published in assorted places, who cycles very slowly for environmental reasons. She is obsessed with trees and chickens. She wrote the poem 'Diagnosis' for her friend, Sally R.

Lori Kiefer writes plays and poetry and is published in various anthologies, including *The Interpreter's House*. She lives in London.

Janet Lancaster writes poems and has been published in several anthologies. She lives in Rutland and has an MA in Creative Writing (Poetry) from Manchester Metropolitan University. She is a member of the Poetry Society's South Leicestershire Stanza. On a good day she may be seen cycling by Rutland Water.

Once, over-excited by her first set of drop handlebars, **Char March** pedalled to warp speed, and ended up with a badly-broken arm between the wheels of an oncoming bus! Char is an award-winning poet whose latest collection *The Thousand Natural Shocks* (Indigo Dreams, 2011) celebrates accidents and mishaps of all sorts.

Alwyn Marriage transported her whole family on a 1931 tandem and sidecar for many years; but she now finds an electric bike is more suitable for tackling the Devon hills and leaves more energy for writing poetry. Some of her work and publications can be seen at www.marriages.me.uk.

Suzanne McArdle is completing her second novel for a Creative Writing MA at Sheffield Hallam University. Her favourite countries to cycle in have so far been Norway and Holland, but she hopes to try others.

Julie Mellor lives in Penistone, near Sheffield, and teaches English at a local secondary school Her poems have appeared in magazines and anthologies, including *Brittle Star*, *Mslexia*, *The Rialto* and *Smiths Knoll*. Her pamphlet, *Breathing Through Our Bones* was published by Smith Doorstop in 2012.

Gail Mosley lives in Leeds but claims to be an Otley-poet-by-association. She began writing in a class at the Courthouse.

James Nash is a writer, poet and long-term resident of Leeds. He has had many short stories published and is currently working on his second novel. In 2012 his selected poems *A Bit of An Ice Breaker*, [an e-book] and a five-star collection, *Some Things Matter*, were published by Valley Press.

Mark Newberry was employed in public service in London before retiring and finding a new life writing verse and songs. Both genres have achieved publication and continue to offer much enjoyment and satisfaction if not much pecuniary profit.

Rennie Parker is published by Shoestring Press, and her next collection is due in 2014. She is also represented on www.poetrypf.co.uk. Her silver Falcon Explorer is very surprised to be the subject of a poem.

Ilse Pedler works as a full time Veterinary Surgeon and has had poems published previously in *Poetry News* and *The North* among others. She usually writes in the car between visits or in bed at night in the half an hour before falling asleep.

Wanda Phillips started writing poetry when she joined Otley Poets and the Poetry Gym. 'After The Night Shift' is her first published poem.

Wendy Pratt lives near Filey, North Yorkshire. Her first collection, *Nan Hardwick Turns into a Hare*, was published by Prolebooks in late 2011 and was well received, being reviewed favourably in the TLS. Her second collection, *Museum Pieces* (2013), was also published by Prolebooks.

Peter Roberts is a lifelong, non-competitive, cyclist. He is rarely happier than when astride a strong sensible bike which he rides wherever life takes him.

Born in Otley, **Michael Shann** now lives in Walthamstow, East London, where he is a member of Forest Poets. His first poetry pamphlet, *Euphrasy*, was published by the Paekakariki Press in 2012 and he has also completed a novel, *The Protesters*, which draws on his experience of living in China. www.michaelshann.com.

Joanna Sedgwick lives in Yorkshire. She has an MA in Interpreting: British Sign language – English from the University of Leeds. Her poems have been published in various magazines and anthologies, including *Magma Poetry* and *The Rialto*.

Steph Shields came late to cycling. Her dad believed bikes dangerous. So it proved. A rusty black bike opened a different world. Her short stories and poems have been published.

Fiona Ritchie Walker is originally from Montrose, Scotland, now living near Newcastle. Her latest poetry collection, *The Second Week of the Soap*, is published by Red Squirrel Press. Follow her on Twitter @guttedherring.

Born in York, **Zoe Walkington** is a keen cyclist and amateur poet. Now living in the Peak District, her passion for cycling up the hills of the national park in a variety of inclement weather conditions inspired her to write 'Mr Pinarello'.

Peter R White left his childhood to spend fifty years as a building services design engineer before joining the Open University to gain a BA (Hons) in Literature and be reborn as a poet. He enjoys meandulating on foot in the hope of enjoying his second childhood with the benefit of experience.

Greg White is a solitary crank who can't handlebars.

As well as being a published writer, **Noel Whittall** is an experienced rider of two-wheelers. He always mounts them from the right.

Rosalind York lives in West Yorkshire where she writes and performs her work. She read Theatre at Dartington and works at a college of further education. The last time she tried to ride a bike she fell off in her next door neighbour's drive.

Acknowledgements

A Perfect Circle by Michael Shann has been published before in his first pamphlet, *Euphrasy* [July 2012], Paekakariki Press (www.paekakarikipress.com).

Drought's End was included in Norman Hadley's self-published collection, *A Whoop Above The Dust*, and was also given an airing on the cycling website he co-edits, www.pedalnorth.com.

Lycra-Clad Loony by Mark Newberry was previously posted online at www.writeoutloud.net.

Madonna of the Pedals by Geraldine Clarkson was previously published in *Marginalia* [2011], Arvon Foundation.

Raleigh Bikes 1976 by Anne Caldwell was previously posted in *Small Word #3* [Sept 2012], www.allographic.co.uk/smallword.

Lightning Star by Carol Ann Duffy was published in *New and Collected Poems for Children* [2009], Faber and Faber Limited.

The dogs that chase bicycles wheels by Ilse Pedler was published in *The North No 50* [2013], The Poetry Business.

A version of **The Oxygen of Words and Wheels** was broadcast on BBC TV and BBC Radio 4, and published in Char March's collection, *The Cloud Appreciation Society's Day Out* [2011], Indigo Dreams.

towpath by James Nash was first published in *Deadly Sensitive* [1999], Grassroots Press, and republished in the Kindle e-book *A Bit of an Ice Breaker* [2012], Valley Press.